Poetic Shadows

Ink and the Sword

Creative Talents Unleashed

GENERAL INFORMATION

Poetic Shadows
Ink and the Sword

By
Creative Talents Unleashed

1st Edition: 2017

This Collection is protected under U.S. and International Copyright laws as a "Collection". All rights for all submissions are retained by the Individual Author and or Artist. No part of this publishing may be Reproduced, Transferred in any manner without the prior **WRITTEN CONSENT** of the "Material Owner" or it's Representative Creative Talents Unleashed.

www.ctupublishinggroup.com

Publisher Information
1st Edition: Creative Talents Unleashed
info@ctupublishinggroup.com

Library of Congress Control Number: 2017931296
Copyright © 2017: Creative Talents Unleashed

ISBN-13: 978-1-945791-18-5 (Creative Talents Unleashed)
ISBN-10: 1-945791-18-7

$12.95

Credits

Book Cover

Raja Williams

Creative Director

D.B. Hall

Editor

Authors Responsible For Own Work

Foreword

L.J. Diaz

Foreword

Thanks to poets and word-weavers such as these, and books such as this, I am incredibly lucky that my reality is shadowed with wonder and fantasy, brimming with adventure and mystery. Too many of us are warriors, fighting our own silent battles with the thought of victory salting our eyes and bringing hope to our battered hearts.

My body has never experienced the grueling determination of a joust, but my heart and mind know all too well the cheers of an excited crowd as my lance perfectly hits the target, knocking my opponent from his horse. And I should probably mention that I've never sat upon a horse. In fact, I'm terrified of them. I've never held a sword in my hands but somehow I know the Siberian and unyielding steel of Excalibur.

I like to think we all possess a touch of fantasy, to some degree. Perhaps our whimsical ways and strange fancies are what make us so very human. We all need to escape from time to time. One of my favorite things to do is to search for rabbit holes and dive right in, feet first, eyes wide open.

Try to imagine a world without fairy tales, imagine a world bereft of magic. What would become of a tender-hearted child's bedtime story? What would happen to the Peter Pan in all of us? Where would the dreamers, the star-child, breathe?

I need magic. You need magic. The world needs magic. I need to believe in everything, not just something. That's me you see - the girl who believes in everything. And I'm more than okay with that. Obviously believing in everything can take its toll. If there aren't monsters under my bed, I can hear them shuffling about inside my closet. And in my dreams, I'm flying, but it's because I'm fleeing fallen angels and demons that want to suck out my soul.

Life is all about taking the bad with the good. Balance is key and timing is everything. When I was young girl I would have happily traded in my cats and dogs for a fire-breathing dragon. Now, when I see a lizard I run away screeching like a bat out of hell.

People tell me dragons don't exist and I laugh in their faces and feel sorry for them and their lack of imagination. I think they may be reincarnated from the ignorant masses who burnt witches at Salem. I fail to see how one cannot be enchanted by witchcraft and all that hocus pocus. It doesn't hurt to live life a little afraid of what you don't know, but when we let fear get a tight grip of us, when we let fear get the better of us, well, that is when we become scared of anything and everything that is different from us, anything that might be a far-cry from a non-fiction existence. That is when we let the magic disappear from our lives, forever.

Who are you? Are you a brave knight? A warrior brandishing your sword, ready for battle. Are you a dreamer? Away with the fairies, losing count of fireflies whilst searching for Neverland. A goth? Who feels right at home with the monsters hiding under the bed, who loves to dance a dervish with the devil on the stroke of midnight. Or perhaps you are a dragon-slayer? Or a soul snatcher? Basking in the heat of an eternal flame. Or maybe you're a witch? Hiding deep in the woods, practicing dark arts beneath the light of a full moon.

L. J. Diaz, Author of Catching Snowflakes

Table of Contents

Foreword   v

Chapter 1 – Of Kings and Knightly Things

The Joust   1
Christopher Allen Breidinger

The Battles of Men   2
Lyne Beringer

Of Sky and Blood (Ode to King Richard III)   3
Ken Allan Dronsfield

Muriel's Moonlit Whispers   4
Justin R. Hart

Home Sickness   6
Janny Bennett

Battle for Vygieskraal   7
Don Beukes

XII   9
Christa Frazee

Fallen and Risen Warrior   10
Ariana R. Cherry

Requiem for a New Hell   12
Ken Allan Dronsfield

Table of Contents

I'll ne'er put one foot in France   13
Mark Andrew Heathcote

Redress   14
Christa Frazee

Diary of an Oracle   15
Don Beukes

A Warrior's Tale: A Faithful Knight In Final Battle   17
Lori Davis

Witch's Cry   19
Amrita Valan

Chapter 2 – Mysterious Magical Things

A Fairy Tale?   23
Susan E. Birch

Memories   24
Maggie Mae Carter

The Land Of Dreams   25
Tammy S. Thomas

Midnight Firefly   26
Elizabeth Daniel

Table of Contents

The Magic Carpet *Vincent Van Ross*	27
Star Child *Janny Bennett*	29
Fluweeltjie *Don Beukes*	30
Stones Echo *D.B. Hall*	32
Minuet of the Ice Fairy *Ken Allan Dronsfield*	33

Chapter 3 – Monsters and Myths

Apollon *Brenda-Lee Ranta*	37
The Weaver and His Quilt *D.B. Hall*	38
Monster of the Night *Debasish Mishra,*	39
Goth Party *Sue Lobo*	40
Fallen Angels *Susan E. Birch*	41

Table of Contents

Porcupine Quills and Ink *Ken Allan Dronsfield*	43
Immersed… *Mark Andrew Heathcote*	44
Truth Stone *Brenda-Lee Ranta*	45
The Beast of Dead Wood – part I *D.B. Hall*	47
Maya-Roona *Valormore De Plume*	49

Chapter 4 – Dragons and Soul Reapers

War Of The Dragons *Tammy S. Thomas*	53
Fire Within *Janny Bennett*	54
Ashes *Anusha VR*	55
Dragon's Fire *Valormore De Plume*	57
Dragon's Dream *Valormore De Plume*	59

Table of Contents

Soul Snatchers *Teresa Roberts*	60
A Red Terror in the Mountains *William Wright, Jr.*	62
Ascension *Lyne Beringer*	63
The Time Dragon *Vincent Van Ross*	65

Chapter 5 – The Woods and the Witches

The Conjurer *William Wright, Jr.*	69
The Witch Doctor *Sue Lobo*	70
MABH *Susan E. Birch*	71
The Lonely Lady in the Red-Hooded Cape *Ariana R. Cherry*	73
The Witchcraft *Vincent Van Ross*	75
The Dark Arts *Lyne Beringer*	77

Table of Contents

Threshold — 79
Justin R. Hart

The Man With the Pitchfork — 81
Teresa Roberts

Under the Full Moon — 83
Maggie Mae Carter

The Spell — 84
Sue Lobo

The Lady at the Round Rustic Table — 85
Ariana R. Cherry

The Witch of the Woods — 87
Debasish Mishra

Dangerous Love: The Knight and The Witch — 88
Tammy S. Thomas

Liberating Luminance — 89
Justin R. Hart

Witches — 91
Teresa Roberts

Epilogue

Starving Artist Fund — 94

CTU Connections — 96

Chapter 1

Of Kings and Knightly Things

The Joust

Upon the steed
The shining silver.
Polish the hooves
And brandish the rods.
Staring down
The clashing river,
They breathe deep
This air of the gods.
Drop the flag,
They shout to heavens.
This confetti gold
The gauntlet's run.
The victor finds
The straightest leaven,
And still upon
His steed, has won.

Christopher Allen Breidinger

The Battles of Men

The master calls his army
To a battle on the field
Marching beasts of burden
No living man can make them yield
They can hear the distant thunder
As silent prayers float toward the clouds
The men who hold the front line
Fall but they never cry out loud
The heavy rain is a welcome friend
Caressing every muddy face
For some it will be the very thing
That floods their resting place
For those that live to tell the tale
Their scars worn with weary pride
Will talk of a battle's glory
How they gave death a hellacious ride
And for every fallen brother
They ask forgiveness for their sins
Speak each man's name in reverence
Who gave their lives so they might live
They'll hold high their swords in unison
A battle braved for all the lost
Knowing hell will be victorious
Souls always end up as the cost
Hail to the brave who've battled
Ten million slaughtered men
On fields with names they never knew
Defying death to the bloody end

Lyne Beringer

Of Sky and Blood ~Ode to King Richard III

Temperance of valor,
greet me with shame
steal away with a sword
from my leather baldric.
Grant me a final wish
before ending my life,
place me upon a throne
with defiant sufferance.
Whilst falling in battle
on a muddy bloody field;
although devout of faith,
whom shall pray for me?
Will your great God above
grant forgiveness for my
sinful murderous contempt?
I am a warrior, not a priest,
tiller of soil; nor a follower
guided along pious paths.
Never forget that haunted
shrill of the battlefield cry.
Proclaim your righteous
virtue, sing your victory
song as sky and blood
drain from my pallid eyes.
As the sounds are muffled
and indistinct, I am suddenly
renewed, feeling a rebirth,
if only in an eternal dream.

Ken Allan Dronsfield

Muriel's Moonlit Whispers

Awareness awoke from the sea's solace;
Muriel's moon energy empathized
with the subsiding tides of emotion,
emoting turmoil of a tortured soul.
So, she mustered a mix of mushroom dust,
sprinkling it over this napping knight's nose.
She fathomed his fear within its ripples
and eased the battle bruised warrior's anguish,
still possessed by his soul seeking struggle.
He could not wash the blood stained memories
of all those whom were killed under his sword.
After so many years of yore's glory,
his dreams were screams of battlefield voices.
Being the best and bravest seemed senseless.
Spanning generations of noble knights,
arrogance had become body fragrance.
Ladies laid lustful Knights as Princes preyed.
Yet, the cosmic fate of our own karmic force
elicits a fair sense of recompense,
as her mind's eye bestowed absolution,
atoning him from his visions of death.
So, into the Knight's ear, she whispered sense:
"Live dignified and worthy of honor
and your presence will be our chosen gift.
Don't merely exist eyeing just our earth;
live life for eternity's remembrance.
Destiny's intent will convey its course
illuminating on your soul's shadow,
bringing ease without your past pride's dis-ease."
The arc-angel warned the worn warrior,
"Unless you learn the lessons in this life,
you will be victim to the same victims.
If you chase the desire of your ego,

you just might catch duality's demon;
Success is when wisdom succeeds conceit.
Focus that pursues purpose on purpose
creates balance to center your insight;
Reasoning the reason of your essence
is to re-focus your own blurred image
with The One reflected upon the pond."
While pondering his exiled existence,
Muriel planted a seed in his dreams
to undertake a dig for deeper depth
than the shallow graves he had left behind.
" 'Till the submissive soil, beyond its leaves
surface, the graves will fill the garden's growth.
Yet, to ascend in the garden you've grown,
simply be blessed by the fruits that are sown."

Justin R. Hart

Home Sickness

Travelling to her home,
Only to find it in ruins.
Her Temple - her people,
Destroyed by humans.
Home sickness sunk in,
As she seen the destruction.
Her glorified Kingdom,
Now looked like a dungeon.

Janny Bennett

Battle for Vygieskraal

In a distant subterranean land far below
the hissing lava lake beyond the whispering
hills of Matroosfontein, a treacherous battle
ground awaits an unknown Bloekomboom
army, awakened by an ancient urgent cry
to prevent eternal annihilation from an enemy
sinister – As the blood from the chaos raging
above drips down to feed the ravenous determined
gamdroelas, each bloekomboom chose a destined
target to hunt down and destroy to save the kingdom
of Vygieskraal, aware that this would be the deciding
final battle to rid the Vygieskraalians once and for all
of this deadly destructive familiar enemy.

With combined power of thought sourced from
essence of tamboerskloof, each bloekomboom
advanced towards clear and charcoal danger – Their
final enemy no distant stranger, for within each damned
gamdroela dwells a fallen disgraced bloekomboom
captured by sangoma magic to destroy their own – The
why and when until now unknown…

As each opponent clashed, the underground grotte shook
and shivered with fallen heroes emanating their given
power in this deciding final hour from a higher order –
Flashes of skaduwees and versteurde echoes of bewende
hesitant relations had no choice but to advance towards the
focal point where all would be revealed in how to ensure a
decisive victory, depending on their heroic last stand to
welcome a necessary outcome grand.

With no obvious escape it was now or nooit, the time has
come to exact the final blow, as each bloekomboom

combined to deliver a spectacular show – Never before has
this been witnessed as each new trunk extended into a
gamdroela darkened heart, extinguishing its cursed essence,
releasing a liberating enchanted shroud to once
again roam freely in a land called Vygieskraal...

Don Beukes

XII

For all you've sweetly done and endured~
I fall deeper in love, over and ever-again…
Forgiving the sinful world, now dormant in you,
As you battle fiercely to protect me from it.

I was abandoned and coldly stranded here~
Untrustingly broken, hiding in the dark woods...
Mocked by poisoned madness and black magic,
And yet, my pain you claimed, calmed...understood.

Piece by piece, you kissed me awake and alive~
Moment by moment, the agonies fell and withered.
In your eyes, I saw a future…then, heaven revealed,
Through your touch, I felt transfixed...purely healed.

Oh, my nobly righteous, romantic King...
You've forged and own the rarest, royal key~
One that so tenderly unlocks my fragile heart…
Protect it, guard it…forever use it, carefully.

My body and honeyed lips, I dedicate to only thee~
My honor and loyalty, is yours for all eternity...
For twelve blessed years, I've been thy blushing Queen~
Adorned with your name, crowned in our precious destiny.

Christa Frazee

Fallen and Risen Warrior

The times had its toll,
The price had been paid.
The warrior entered in,
fought with a brittle heart,
but then exited
with a fearful grace....

She walked along a rocky road
under a bright glowing moon
and her long hair flowed lightly
as it danced in the cool breeze.

The warrior felt her way through a lonely darkness
With her head held high and tear-stained eyes.
She stayed focused, even though, her favorite star had burnt
out. She marched on.

There were more steps to be trod,
As each one was lit up from the glow of the high crescent
moon. Twas a dark and rocky path the warrior traveled
In the bleak autumn evening, Faint lights flickered as she
passed through isolated and desolate streets.

The warrior was determined to create a new onward
moment. She marched on. A heart of scars built with
uneven emotional lines, yet the warrior marched on.

Her soul, portrayed a strong-willed warrior.

She tries to live the life that has been destined.
A spirit attacked from the now and then. With her guard,
she plans for the war of the future.
She marches on...

A warrior.
A warrior whose heart was attacked, whose soul was beaten, but has a spirit that is lifting…

She owns the night and marches on.

Ariana R. Cherry

Requiem for a New Hell

Blame me not of a heartless vengeance
inked words nor intolerable pestilence
a keeper of life's incandescent tolerance
mocked by the icy queried inquisitions.
Steamy breath within pious incantations
raucous mind of a boiling incessant joy
home in purgatory, refuge within evil
I'm not afraid to walk this world alone.
In dungeons of a darkish desperation
percolating a new hell from deep within
roaming the covenant on ancient paths
uncovering graves of the fallen saints.
Battlements and those gated horrors
in bunkers of suicidal choreography
saltpeter and brimstone explode in envy
seeing the stars within eternal darkness.
Written in the sky with a neon yellow ink
missing the blood moon in all her glory.
The question isn't "who will allow me life"
but rather, "who shall try to stop me?"

Ken Allan Dronsfield

I'll ne'er put one foot in France

… Ladies, I've observed the eternal night
Dressing up these shadows bathed in starlight
But with every footstep taking its rightful place
Monitoring, you at a snail's pace.

Something, I couldn't begin to equate…
Kept me dragging my heels earthly weight
As you glided along with moonlight interlace
I, couldn't chart the stars you'd, far too much grace.

As I am neither a chivalrous knight
Nor my Lady of this intrepid ghostly night
Am I a saint, as I am just a Paige of the lance
I'll ne'er put one foot in France
… But prays me, I'll find my own, sunny romance.

Mark Andrew Heathcote

Redress

Purple heart in agonized amethyst~
Throbbing theatrics and a tongue undone...

Hooded cape of bloodied, bold scarlet~
Shielding a pale face of tears from the sun...

Muddied black boots and a dragging lace hem~
Stomping towards the beckoning battlefield...

The melancholy Maiden returns, to spite them,
Wielding her sharpened sword and painted shield...

Rich theatrics of the storming, old soul~
Full of pained vengeance, once peaceful sweetness...

She insists upon this tragic throne of retribution~
For the fairytale turned morbid, through carelessness.

Christa Frazee

Diary of an Oracle

Sekueb Nodmai – Wisdom is not bestowed on just any inherited ancient crown but one such king is what the stones have predicted eons ago – No amount of dark spells whispered by cursed wretched vindictive elves could prevent his imminent foretold crowning – As the subjects of his kingdom were slowly morally drowning, he alone could make them atone for even sins unknown – Great was his task to unite three war-torn kingdoms at last and restore royal order after viscious centuries of failed fatal missions and blurred horrid visions – Now began a new era with echoes of a people spreading their desperate cry to a monarch known as His Eminence, Sekueb Nodmai…

Eniamrahc – A royal maiden, her foretold mission no more hidden – A newly crowned ruler revealing his fatherly instruction to claim her birthright secret from a legendary elusive oracle – A liberating legendary key to everlasting life from a watery source to avoid an earthly grave but behold the others chosen from kingdoms magically frozen – Each now on a maiden journey instructed to seek and find the enigmatic elected oracle to show the way to eternal life's miracle – Armed with ancient secret herbs, Eniamrahc had no choice but to embark on this perilous journey – Crossing the fiery plains of Vygieskraal with her mystical veil shielding her from the deadly snarling gamdroelas, her human stench masked by root of knoffel dug out from the ancient wortel tree – Moving stealthily towards the secret waterfall, guided by the soothing song of the kwêvoël to reach the sanctuary of the oracle…

The Revelation – As Eniamrahc approached her destination she found herself compelled towards an ancient wisdom, radiating from an expectant oracle – Reveal to me your secret ingredient and I will gift you what you seek to prove your expected obedience, said the oracle without moving her revelatory mouth – Oh revered oracle I have for you extract of waterblommetjie infused with breath of tokkelossie, now please show me the way to the prophesized archway there to find the key to what I seek – The mystical egg of the treasured gansvoël – I am convinced by your precious herbal gift, so follow my voice and your kingdom will eternally rejoice oh daughter of Sekueb Nodmai.

Don Beukes

A Warrior's Tale: A Faithful Knight In Final Battle

Your Knights we beseech thee in earnest Lord.
We hear the beckon cry forlorn.
Of peasants and the village men,
all bellowing in times gone dark and grim.
We sense the faltering of our fortified might,
of the rampart walls from which we fight.
We sense a turbulence deep within,
and question valor and the whim.
Of nation states who do'eth wryth,
in bloodshed battles amidst our cries.
Across the valleys and this fortress mote,
we see a future of which you've spoke.
A grand and sensitive valley plain,
where honor's legacy doth never wane.
Valor is tested in century time,
and like all medieval memories,
lives in a heart like mine.
I feel the gothic creaking tale,
of noble Lords and people frail.
Who crumble under falling board,
of castle wall and battle sword.
We Knights of sacred destiny known,
we enter this rock and vest our valor this morn.
As the sun doth rise across the plain,
we gather our might and we gather our pain.
Tomorrow we beckon our knights around,
and enter the enemy without a sound.
With the quick of a draw
the knife blade quivers,
and with the whisper of the edge,
the enemy doth shiver.

Poetic Shadows – Ink and the Sword

Like the blade of summer grass,
some nations mend.
And, so to this,
this day, we end.
Our legacy now fortified but with bloodlines deceased,
I question who is the hero and who is the beast.
And though I now wonder in winter's rain,
Now only a spirit of this great plain,
I am haunted by the raven's cry.
The day I laid down my sword,
the day I died.

Lori Davis

Witch's Cry

Amelie, I am still here
Still waiting, my pretty dear
Out in this brazen blizzard
Under this beautiful sky painting's
Midnight blue false ceiling
With wisps of white trimming
Wishful will o' the wisp wind
works it's wanton wanderings
Calls to thee my heart
Whispering my soul's secrecy
Here Amelie!
Hear me.
The graveyard shift
Churns my callow blood.
My goose pimpled skin
Is hung out like a shroud
Slicing this reality machine
That blinds ye.
Amelie, you were my little girl.
The unborn baby
Macabre sacrifice.
You're my everything
Witchcraft in the wind
Spells too sacred to tell.
You're the reason
I wield a wand.
My child.
Your carcass strung
Over the cauldron
As the coven
Made demand.
The covenant was made.

Purest holiest blood shed
I am now working all the mirrors
Of the universe.
And shattering crystals
That cry out
Baying bloodthirsty moons
You're not dead my child
While I live
My eyes agonized
Shards of bloodbath...
Amelie your epitaph
Marks the Tombstone
Of my soul.
I am not alive.
A witch lies encrypted
Between life and death
Love and hate
Bewitched.
Missing you
Kissing you
Messing with your hair
Thank you for the memories.
The haunting insight of humanity
Tendered for sale.
Those are my roots
I swing alone
Between Nictitating
Night vision
And Necromancer
Netherlands.

Amrita Valan

Chapter 2

Mysterious Magical Things

A Fairy Tale?

In a time before time
When Earth was one great forest
Encompassing oceans,
An elder race,
Gifted for their devotions,
Became the guardians
Of all that is
And all that was.

When man strove to understand his place,
To know and learn of Nature and Earth
They took our hand, gave us grace
To glimpse our true potential worth,
And return that love in equal part
From a self-fulfilling heart.
And so we did
And so it was.
Alas, we then betrayed their trust
And, to our eternal shame,
Forgot the love and learned to lust
For what was never ours to claim.

Earth and Nature became a game
Of thrones and borders never crossed.
Earth was defiled
And Heaven lost.

Susan E. Birch

Memories

The Earth remembers
When magic was high
The Air remembers
When dragons flew by

The humans tell fables
Not remembering why
Maybe they are unable
Only Magic knows why

Days when fairies danced
In the wood
Nights when witches
Did not need a hood

The Sun and Moon
Are biding their time
For when dragons return
The Magic will dine

Maggie Mae Carter

The Land Of Dreams

As I drift off into Dreamland
My mind began to play
I see unicorns and elves
Dancing their hearts away
Witches racing on their brooms
Casting spells to meet your doom
Leprechauns wants to trade,
gold for your soul and stay
In dreamland forever
I must say you're clever
But to stay I can never!
So I flew on a fairy far away
as I could, deep in the woods
and lost never to be found

Tammy S. Thomas

Midnight Firefly

As midnight's fog
Wraps the world in gray
Mischief makers tiptoe
Through brambles and crunching twigs
Tiny elves of magic
Invisible to the naked eye
Appearing only as a firefly.

Elizabeth Daniel

The Magic Carpet

Jane had just lost her parents
In an accident
A few days ago
And, all her relative
Were gathered at her place
To decide as to what is to be done
With the property left behind
By her wealthy parents

Janes parents knew how greedy
Their relatives were
They had foreseen this situation
When they were still alive

So, they took Jane to the attic
When she turned twelve
And showed her a magic carpet
That would fly away at her command

As Jane's uncles and aunts
Stood there discussing about
Who would get what
Out of the legacy
Jane was totally disgusted
And she wanted to teach
Her relatives a lesson

So, she had the magic carpet
Brought over to the dining room
And had it spread on the floor
Then she got the dining table
And the chairs in place
Then she went on

To set up the dinner
On the dinner table

Once the dinner was ready
She invited all her relatives to dinner
Once all of them were seated
She stepped back into the adjoining room
And commanded the magic carpet
To fly away to a distant land
From where her relative
Could never return to bother her

The magic carpet flew away
With all her relatives
Saving Jane and her property
From the greedy eyes
Of her relatives

Vincent Van Ross

Star Child

Be proud of yourself,
You've come a long way
- From where it all first begun.
Swimming upstream,
Just to try your luck.
Never giving up,
Because the ordinary
- Was just never enough!
Now hold your head high,
And spread Stardust!

Janny Bennett

Fluweeltjie

Beneath Table Mountain beyond where two oceans meet lies a hidden place only those who unlock the secret entrance can ever hope to see, a place filled with devious enchanted reverie by a horde of fantastic creatures some with eye-popping weird features but be not afraid and patiently wait for your elected sign to attempt to enter their congregational shrine – For this is the ancient land of Fluweeltjie where only a selected few is granted the opportunity to uncover its secrets divine –

You might just be aware of a delicate creature with a peculiar stare as you wander on an unfamiliar path hoping to find your way back to the start, it might even seem to know your name but be vigilant as it lures you to its secret lair with hissings of magical grandeur for it is the rare korrelkop, a devious little konyn chosen to trick you into a sense of euphoria as you search for an imagined utopia so heed to the warning sound of the babbling brook as it gently crashes over a watery nook predicting a familiar old trick for if you follow the false trail you will end up as a minion for the self-elected klong – From who you will never be set free so hurry and flee for this is the land of Fluweeltjie.

Distant strange drumming might signal your untimely coming or is it the thundering of crashing waves below hiding their celebratory dancing as yet another unsuspecting victim has fallen for the ancient trap set each mercury full moonlight following a strange light bright but not quite, for it draws you closer with enchanted notes enveloping you – Welcome hands carrying you as you submit to their harp-like voices for they are the feared

fallen mannemerak who chose to get stuck in a watery
grave trying to retrieve the irresistible tasting
perlemoen healing plant – Now they feed on you instead
and have their celebratory nightly reverie in this strange
place called

Fluweeltjie...

Don Beukes

Stones Echo

Back when elves built magical wonderlands in trees
And the music of the bards drifted upon the breeze
Beautiful faeries threw parties late into the night
Gaiety of laughter signified everything was alright

Elders had a charge to curate the sacred archives
But were pulled from their scrolls by their needy wives
Out onto earthen dance floor to the sounds of lyre
Being bumped and jostled amid trees alit by faerie fire

Mugs and cisterns are full of that ancient Elvin ale
Aged for centuries in a process that they would tell
Always try the Brownie's Stane; but don't over pour
Around the pole, grab the ribbons let spirits soar

Kinsman magic protecting and illuminating the night
Stones of Callanish will echo fun till morning's light

D.B. Hall

Minuet of the Ice Fairy

Ravens sing in a shrill harmony
flying above the red fiery pyre.
Sprite-lings fly dodging snow;
seeking boughs of cedar cover.
Ice fairies waltz a loving minuet
on a clear ice crystal snowflake.
Goblins dress in Sunday attire;
soft kisses with lemonade pouts,
awaiting all those sordid desires.
Love the cherished mystical soul
whilst misty diamond stars weep.
During that icy passionate dance,
scarlet blood shall rise and steep.
Flashing tease of an ocular ellipse,
peeking full moon in pastel clouds.
Edge of a cold goblins rapaciousness
inhales of a pinkish twilight unicorn,
all enjoy the Minuet of the Ice Fairy.

Ken Allan Dronsfield

Poetic Shadows – Ink and the Sword

Chapter 3

Monsters and Myths

Apollon

Standing in a temple, his
Apollon of symbolic love,
a soldier of one guarding
his mythical idealisms
Daphne approaching the
sacred ground, awareness
not awe inspiring, not even
a trifle, a fearful, painful void
serendipity or revelry not, be
only empty echoes in the night,
be it a thought, a dream, a wish.
if none hear the sound of its voice
it is but a whisper, like the wind
holding its mouth agape, meaning
nothing, soundless, when it be
only solitary sound of the esoteric
while the lyre played on and on,
none be audible from the Delphic
Daphne whirled, whirled, spinning,
swaying to silent music of the gods
that was only
meant for her,
never to hear
she was pained
she was relieved
an outline of the temple
now barely visible
was fast becoming
Apollon's tomb and
Daphne's memory

Brenda-Lee Ranta

The Weaver and His Quilt

Legends of old
foretold your coming
so the jealous Weaver hatched a plan
daring and bold
luminescence was stolen from a million stars
and woven with magic into a matchless quilt
decorated with windowpane oyster shells
and priceless pearls
in a vain attempt to match the brilliant shine
of your imminent beauty.

Innocent and unaware you came
stroding boldly through the pounding surf
whitecaps splashed in ecstatic glee
against your smooth olive skin
the wind whipping your wild alabaster hair
a natural love of life
flashing from those glorious green eyes.

Upon being bathed in your presence
the Weaver immediately knew he had failed
that with each confident stride you took
he was losing turf so The Weaver offered up his quilt
as a gift to robe you and cover your pristine nakedness.

Once this immaculate quilt was clasped around your neck
and gathered in your hands
beauty and magic united sparkled and swirled
dipped and swayed until you arose to eternal majestic
heights and so The Moon was born.

D.B. Hall

Monster of the Night

When darkness swells
In the dead of the night,
And an eerie silence hangs in the air,
I see that enormous Creature crawling,
Monstrously, inch by inch, towards me!

It's dangerous for sure;
I can sense the venom in its tongue,
The fire in its eyes,
The strength in its sinews!
It is more dangerous
Than what probably Yeats had seen!

Like the embodiment of Leviathan,
Or the huge Atlas, it comes
Unhindered in its purpose, ruthlessly
Fluttering the shining sword,
Grinding it's jaws with bitter rage!

As the distance dwindles, I fear
The size and the enormity,
A hundred dinosaurs fused into one,
Desperate to destroy the world.

I swallow a gulp and nervously ask,
"Who are you, O Monster?
What do you want?"
The deadpan face engenders a smile,
A brutal smile, when He chuckles,
"I am War, my friend. I'll efface everything."

Debasish Mishra

Goth Party

You're cordially invited to a party by the ancient black Goth, where you'll be lit by the moonlight & escorted by the moth, held in the cloisters of the graveyard, by the old tombstones, where grey dank mists are stirred by the old cracked bones.

Be garbed in alabaster pore & draped in gown of midnight lace, inked scarlet lip & ebony eye, shall mask your mysterious face, please come grave-ash-booted by the light of the haunted moon, and old medieval chanting's, by black ravens shall dance the tune.

By eerie yellow candlelight & on bat broth, you shall gaudily dine, you shall quaff from bloody gargoyle goblet, full rich garnet wine, Serpents from the Styx shall dance & skulls will wink & slyly smile, and midnight cavorting shall excite loins & seduce the ready bile.

You'll be serenaded all night by hounds & wolves that bay & howl, kissed upon your powdered cheek by the flitting bat & hooting owl, you shall dance the night away, with spiders in their webs of dew, until the glinting of dawn appears & washes the fresh day anew.

I'm sending you this invitation to a party, of the midnight Goth, if you accept, the folk of the night, to you, their hats shall doff, so don your glad rags, those black, dark & of deep velvet hue, and there shall surely be a dark & eerie welcome awaiting you.

Sue Lobo

Fallen Angels

Once we were the prime elect,
The chosen and select few.
Our duty? To teach and defend.
To that end we were armed with might.
The boundless skies were our reward
And light from sun, moon and star
Fuelled our magical flight.
Duty bound, we laboured long .
Taught earthbound kin right from wrong,
Respect for Earth and each other
Soul to Soul..sister and brother.
Earth, man and us in harmony
Equilibrium achieved.
A galactic melody.
Alas, often we turned our eyes
From Earth and man to seek the skies.
But Oh! how the stars sang to us!
As we blindly turned our face
The moon bathed us in her grace
And the mighty sun's living flow
Did paint us in his timeless glow.
In our hubris we did neglect
To ever serve and to protect.
Declared ourselves a special sect.
We were favoured! We owned the skies!
And man diminished in our eyes
Our final act...our greatest sin
We judged them as a lesser kin.
Their brief short lives we proudly scorned,
Their fate and Earth's by us unmourned.
In our folly and conceit
We had claimed ourselves elite
And sang our cosmic song.

Ah! How wrong we were.
We did not see the bitter seeds
We sowed, nor the harvest we were owed.
We neglected our earthbound kin far too long
Who, in their ignorance, found another song
And sang and sang until the blood ran.
Misguided, they plundered earth and sea.
Their only gods were 'I' and 'ME'.
The universe wept!
And we were swept
Into a cosmic storm,
Our wings ripped and torn!
Our infamy at last repaid
Cast to the Earth we had betrayed.
Those who managed to survive
Saw the Hell allowed to thrive
And wept with shame.
This, now, was ours....this dark domain.

Susan E. Birch

Porcupine Quills and Ink

Put my grave atop the great waterfall;
wrap me well inside my favorite blanket
place my bow and arrow upon my chest
put my headdress of Bald Eagle feathers
on my head and lay me on a bed of fern
leave me in peace, staring off at the sky
now turning a deep red at twilight's call
feed my pony grains coated with honey
he must wait until the great one calls him.
tell my family that I died with honor and
my only regret is not being there this cold
fall and winter to provide food and firewood.
yes, put me on the wood, atop the waterfall.
mark my name on a tall swamp cedar pole
use porcupine quills and inks in my pouch
light the fire and watch me fly into the sky!

Ken Allan Dronsfield

Immersed…

The night is a nicotine patch.
A burnish of black leather…
A bleeding scratch
…On a naked nether.

It is altogether a womb,
Some giants, eyelid blinking
A mammoth's, bog, tomb…
Glinting of times, eroding.

Sleep navigates its marshes
Through – nightmare—forest.
Crawling into reeds, sedges
Standing, fearfully deforest.

Legs trembling—in coyness
Light is again touched
And rousingly it is loved
Immersed in a new, mistress.

Mark Andrew Heathcote

Truth Stone

a coveted moonstone secreted by
her corseted bosom, lay against her
heart, her long tendrils fell upon ivory
shoulders, her onyx eyes – challenging.
pulling golden sabre from it's sheath
making ready to spar for a sacred stone.
the other, his emblazoned breast plate,
glints of a lunar light; raising his sword
for her honour alone, a duel to win her;
she be the prize, she be his true magic

when chalice shall hold their blood,
raised on high victorious, a wench,
beauteous in mystery, love bitten in
a singular glance, shaking her mane
of silken hair, haughty, enticing him
that be privy alone to her favours,
whilst steeds be stepping back in
readiness of the riders call, to the
death, be it moonstone, be it she,
their contest be jousting - taunting

behind a thicket, she slipped in wait
her future on steeds, their mighty
wails of chivalry decreed, keeping
her pride at bay, knowledge that for
him, a coveted stone be the prize,
whilst the other saw only her, a
Bellibone, in her simple perfection.
a silence followed by crackling of
twigs beneath each footfall, breath
quickened; her eyes snapped open

he stood before her, the glint of a
breastplate, his arms extended out
towards her, beckoning, his hand
opened, in his palm a glistening
moonstone; she, pulling out same
blue stone, hidden in her bosom;
held it out to him too, a battle won
for her alone, philotimy was hers,
she forever the victory, she never
be the spoils, beseeching his love

they made haste to each other's arms,
cling to each other, his low mutterings
"Oh fair one, let me die before you,"
his body falling slowly to the ground,
to lay among the leaves in the thicket;
his moonstone fell at her feet; blue glint
of lunar light reflected in his armour,
a garnet pool forming beneath him;
onyx rained from her eyes, magic lost,
her moon had perished beneath the stars

two moonstones lay betwixt them in the
evening dew, reflecting nothing at all.

Brenda-Lee Ranta

The Beast of Dead Wood – part I

There was no singular moment
that I noticed when breezes stopped
or when birds no longer sang
and squirrels hid in attics of trees.

For I had wandered totally enraptured
lost within my poetic thoughts
until I crossed the threshold into the dead wood
a forbidden place
where no one dared to venture
for once they did
they never returned
another gruesome victim
of the legendary beast of the dead wood.

Panicked, I raced back
to find my way out
but every way seemed to just
lead me into denser darker wood
intertwining branches loomed over me
an enveloping canopy cutting off air
making it unbearably despondent.

Silhouetted trunks spoke with no sound
voices of souls long since dead
with a mocking laugh welcoming me
to an eventual moss-covered grave.

The complete absence of sound and beauty
was such a rude awakening
it gave birth to a rise of heightened primal fear
and changing anomalies
breeding in a hyper-fertile mind.

Seconds were days
furtive eyes darted into every shadow
heightened senses analyze every crevice
I raced through an ever-changing maze
tripping over roots alive and moving
landing face-first through mud and decaying leaves
jumping up and falling down
until
digits
hands
limbs
and coverings
slowly adapted in desperation and protection
until man finally became beast.

Various walls of dark caves
echo my haunting howls
they contain my desolate scribblings
scratched with claws that can hold no pen
I am cursed and hunted by villagers
that used to be my neighbors and family.

I have become the beast of the dead wood
a curse upon my soul.

D.B. Hall

Maya-Roona

Eerie sounds present themselves, on such a night as this.
Beneath the ample harvest moon, they wander in the mist,
creeping as they lick the hairs, while tingling up your spine.
Trembling hands serve not well, withering courage, on the
vine.

Darkened forest shadows splinter moonbeam's glow,
as figments infiltrate your mind. Allocate the fleshy
curtains to drape around your eyes, entice your ears to find,
the way to Grandma's house. You could follow the winding
path, even if you're blind. Smell the hemlock as you pass
the mushroom patch, beyond the melon's rotting rind.

Think naught, nor linger long, on the vicious creatures,
seeking a nocturnal meal, nor of their matted furriness, nor
claws, nor pointy teeth, though they are quite real.
Remember the bony bones, protruding from the ooze that
once you thought were logs. Strain to listen wisely, for the
bubbling methane, as you near the putrid bogs.

Hasten from rock to rock, whilst skipping across the
stream, lest eerie eels pull you down and make you want to
scream. Wake not the Maya-Roona; you know her from
your dream, the serpent from the quagmire with reddish
eyes that gleam.

Do not let fall your shield, neither dare to shed a tear,
and do not mislay the gift, you brought for granny dear.
Keep your wits about you and your cutlass at your side,
for now you're in the open, with no safe place to hide.

Each hungry creature's eyes are, upon your pulsing throat.
Although you're running faster, it's not the time to gloat.

Poetic Shadows – Ink and the Sword

Sly old Maya-Roona slithers, near your Granny's bed,
you can only kill her, when your sword removes her head.

Do not tarry, listening to, her impassioned hiss. Verily,
she's craving more, than just a little kiss. When you draw
close to Granny, look round about again. Be sure it's your
dear Granny, not Maya-Roona's grin.

She overshadows your mind, while spinning endless lies,
comprehension left behind, beneath red ember eyes. Be you
most certain to note, the number of the day. Three days,
centered on the thirteenth, Granny goes away.

What is it Granny does here to fill her deepest needs?
You've heard the horrid stories, accounts of evil deeds.
Haven't you wondered why, Granny lives in forest deep,
or of your excursions, where monsters do surely creep?

Think back to lore about, Maya-Roona's evil ways.
Recollect the accounting of Maya-Roona's days.
Centered on the thirteenth, Maya-Roona comes for prey.
Granny, is the Maya-Roona, so the people say.

Valormore De Plume

Chapter 4

Dragons and Soul Reapers

War Of The Dragons

Tonight we fight!
The kingdom we must save
Gather all the knights, horses, and their armor
Our land we must defend thy honor
We must attack before the dragons awakens
Off with their heads, we will be taken
Destroying our homes with fire no more!
Knights strike the dragons with thy swords!

Tammy S. Thomas

Fire Within

There was no way,
The dragon could stay.
Luring girls,
To his hideaway.
Scaly and green,
He ordered her to obey.
So she picked up a sword,
And battled him anyway.
Far from brave,
She fought this day.
She stabbed him in the heart,
And slayed a dragon…
- Right into his grave!

Janny Bennett

Ashes

The dragon soared across the night sky
Looking down upon the passers by.

She thirsted for the blood of a knight
For the first times in weeks he had slipped out of her sight.

Before she had been a black-scaled monster,
She had been a princess, a sister, a daughter.

But that was eons ago, when love had tricked her heart
His facade had made her believe they would never be apart.

One night in the woods, a curse had been cast
The world believed she was dead, she became a thing of the past.

He played the role of the grieving widower to perfection
The royal family had fallen prey to his deception.

Into the thick woods, slipped the knight.
She followed the trail flooded with moonlight.

Towards the witch's hut he scurried
to embraced the wretched woman he had married.

The king had given away his treasures
Which they could now spend at leisure.

Their love would no longer be a secret
Once they left the kingdom without a fret.

The shadows came alive all of a sudden,
The black dragon emerged from where she was hidden.

Golden flames unfurled from the belly of the beast.
Everything turned to ash as the sun heralded a new day from the east.

Anusha VR

Dragon's Fire

We are solitary predators
battling to the death over territory.
Females are smaller although,
more cunning and fierce.
The mating season is fraught with peril,
as lethal adversaries assess prospects.
The male must fly on his back,
vulnerable to the female's option to couple or kill.
Her scent fills the breeze from the north
as she hides in the shelter of sinister clouds.
To surprise her would encourage opposition;
my swelling desire for her must be patient.
When first you soar across the lunar fullness,
your silhouette set the flame within me to writhe.
Cold silver light shines through your wings,
exposing your faultless femininity.
I stride upon the gentle wind,
while pursuing you through the darkness.
Eyes lend unconvincing assistance,
in the hollow black clouded night sky.
Silken swirls hasten through your beautiful scales,
betraying you not.
Elegant wings arrange silent slices of the night,
to carry you aloft.
Heart throbbing within your breast,
brings focus to target my quest.
We dragons court in extreme fashion,
for delight and wrath, both light our fires.
You will embrace me for your passionate desires,
or slay me for a whim.
Drawing near, you feel my hot breath
as this night starts in love, yet may end in death.
Your claws scrape me in pay back

as I thrust in to possess you.
Interlaced with one ember's sweet burn,
we plummet with radiant colors.
You capture my pride to assimilate my essence,
a prisoner to your love, as you decide our destiny.
The terrain below rushes nearer,
as our passion intensifies to fulfillment.
Our destiny becomes apparent,
as we break off toward our separate territories.
I return to my lofty perch, reminisce of brief ecstasy
and savor the memory of holding you close.

Valormore De Plume

Dragon's Dream

Bluegreen eyelids hover halfway cross v-shaped pupils,
as they descend to conceal fiery ambergris eyes.
Dragons worry little of men and elfish scruples,
for the millenniums of enchanted living make them wise.

The fairies flutter round about on iridescent lavender wings,
playing hide-n-seek between his teeth and many pointy horns.
Dragon's off to dreamland where his long-gone lover sings,
she was the fairest beauty ever took to sky, til that dreadful morn.

They'd race near grasses in the valley low, soar the mountains above,
through the darkest forests, and beneath the ocean's waves.
He was the only male to fertilize the flock, although she was his only love.
The females live a shorter life, and now they're in their graves.

His wings feel rather tattered now, when he takes to air.
He hunts the men he feeds upon easily while prancing on his legs.
Then he returns to the comfort of the cavern to dream of his lady fair,
just him and all the fairies, to watch over thousands of purple eggs.

Valormore De Plume

Soul Snatchers

He saw the shadow on the wall
many years ago
It was long and tall
Looming over his bed
But when he mentioned it
to his mom and dad
They said it was all in his head

So he took their word as children do
And went his merry way
He wasn't certain through and through
But over time he did forget
about that shadow strange
And could laugh at other's stories
without a smidgeon of regret

Until the day the shadow play
graced his grownup world
Dark and menacing at the end of day
With fanged smile and cape unfurled
Holding him hostage with the intention
of stealing his soul by bloodletting
and other things he couldn't mention

Yes, he went willingly into the night
As he watched his life slip away
Becoming a tiny speck of light
There was no cursing or flailing about
It was painless from the start
He simply let the shadow steal
His vision and his heart

The next morning was almost the same

as all the days before
He could not give the change a name
as he walked out the door
heading down a street thus lined
with hordes of soulless people
whose lives the shadow had defined.

Children understand
Dogs may, too
That the shadows of the undead
are real and full of dread
And what they saw upon their wall
was never in their heads at all.

Teresa Roberts

A Red Terror in the Mountains

A mountain flares to life
With the rolling blaze
Of a beastly curse

Serpentine
He glows with crimson scales
Enraged
At the steel-plated swarms
In their thundering assault

They are meant
To spare what remains
Of the scorched sprawl of home
Their ever-green shires
In despair

The beast
He blares his wrath
As the armored unsheathe and storm
And savagery, boils in their blood

They charge into the fray
And are tragically engulfed
In bound, for eternity's embrace

The serpent prevails once more
And claims the broad skies
From the bare blackened trees
That crumble, cascade, and weep

William Wright, Jr.

Ascension

He was predisposed toward pandering
A predator of the dark
I heard he was known by many names
But he preferred the term "The Shark"
He approached me in the evening
Just as the city came to life
His face half hidden in a hoodie
In his hand was a pocketknife
I stood there in the silence
As he looked me up and down
I could swear I saw him smiling
A passing car now the only sound
My feet were lightly tapping
As I stood there on the street
Then I heard him whisper
I'm thrilled we finally got to meet
He said he'd been here waiting
For me to find my way
To the place he kept well hidden
From the heat and the light of day
I've kept your chamber frozen
The floors thick with sheets of ice
Magic mirrors are on the ceiling
So you can see your reflection twice
I thanked him for his service
But a century's past in years
I have hungered for the taste of it
Lost souls paralyzed with fear
So I summoned all the shadows
Inhaled his screams as they gathered round
The shark that once was dangerous
Disappeared without another single sound
Now I feel their presence

Those who languish in the in-between
Destiny is calling
It's the ascension of the Arctic Queen

Lyne Beringer

The Time Dragon

In deep sleep
I felt as if I was being
Clawed and tugged
By a dragon to wake me up
I kept sleeping
And, drifted into a dream

I found a dragon
Staring at me
In place of eyes
It had two clocks
And, on the snout,
It had a third clock

The dragon told me
That it was the time dragon
And it could take me out
On time travel

The Time Dragon also told me
That it could take me to the past,
The present
Or, the future

'Where are we, right now?'
I asked
We are in the present replied the dragon

I have three clocks on my face
Two of them are where my eyes ought to be
And the third one is on my snout

One of these clocks light up
According to the time zone we are in

When the clock on my snout lights up
It means we are in the present
When the one on my left eye lights up
It means we are in the past
And when the one on my right eye lights up
It means we are in the future

The entire universe is in a time warp

The past is buried under the ground
It is in the nether world
The present is on the ground
It is on the earth
And, the future is in the air
It is in outer space

Time travelers
Can switch
From one time zone to the other
Because, in the universe,
The past, the present and the future
Exist at the same time

And, I am the time dragon
That can take you
To any of them
At your command…

Vincent Van Ross

Chapter 5

The Woods and the Witches

Poetic Shadows – Ink and the Sword

The Conjurer

Shielded by the dead of night
A homestead is alight
With neon-colored potions and plans

A lone and crooked frame
Weaves back and forth
Through the nurturing silence

Where his madness may grow
Into an outburst of genius
Where his cauldrons ignite
And froth with his loathsome schemes

Until, "the night has come"
Crawls out of his throat
And a dream, becomes a world set ablaze
A triumph, left smoldering in his past

William Wright, Jr.

The Witch Doctor

He lives in thatched hut, deep within the African bush, where beasts die of thirst & vultures swoop in a whoosh, his hut is dark & hot & smells of roots, herbs & bloody pelts, and in his three legged cauldron, his potions he duly smelts.

Hanging from wooden rafters, are the gruesome animal parts, he chants words of magic, over bones, livers & pulsating hearts, ancient potions & unguents, mixed with entrails, reeking of smoke, while frantically dancing round his fire & to old spirits he invokes.

With all his wild chanting, prancing & trancing, he tosses old bones, calling to his ancient ancestors, buried beneath old rocks & stones, with the sacrifice of poor beasts, he swears oaths & pleads to the Gods, for the powerful magical mixing of herbs, from the earth's given clods.

He lifts bestowed curses, with dried hide, claw, mighty talon & horn, massaging old wrinkled bodies with balsams of old powdered thorn, telling the young, for love, to imbibe, poison & hideous snake's blood, for stings & bites, to rub in well, the fat of hippo & the delta's black mud.

To call rare rain, he rattles pods of baobab & old desert's singing seeds, collected & gathered at full moon, by the place of the crocodile's reeds, and when I visit the old witchdoctor's hut, deep in the dark African bush,
Seeking my future, looking up I see, the old vulture swoop with a whoosh.

Sue Lobo

MABH

Cold moonlight bathes the forest scene
The Court of Faere doth now convene
In wildest witchwood gathered there
To praise the fairest of the Faere.

Step lightly stranger in this place.
Show reverence.... an act of grace
Toward these ancient, sacred ways
Recorded in the book of days.

She who rules the hearts of Fae,
The Lords and Ladies, Tuatha De',
Stands astride the Web of Wyrd
She, whom even ancients feared,

She is La Belle Dame sans Merci
Queen and ruler of the Sidhe
Who does not suffer easily
Such mortal fools as we may be.

Some whisper that she has no soul,
Others say her soul is old.
Queen of War and Wolven Queen,
Queen of Poets, Queen of Dreams.

She can withhold or grant desires
With spells she weaves of eldritch fires,
Lightning storms and moonbeam's gleam.
She can make or break your dream.

Step not within the oaken round
But 'neath the Rowan's hallowed ground
In truth, your heart and soul relate,

Make your wish and seal your fate.

Angel with a devil's wiles,
Devil with an angel's smiles.
She is not judged, yet judges she
And, on a whim, she will decree....
...and as She wills
So mote it be.

Susan E. Birch

- Pronunciation

- Mabh - Maeve.
- Tuatha De' - Tooha Day
- Sidhe - Shee
- Fae - Fay)

The Lonely Lady in the Red-Hooded Cape

A bright full moon shines upon high, into a starless night. Clouds float slowly through the darkness, finding their way through a fog.

Into the silent of the moon-lit night, a wolf's emotional howl is heard, echoing through the icy breeze, sending chills down the spine of anyone who hears.

Down below, onto the earthly land, a dark haired middle-aged woman dressed in a red-hooded cape stands outside an old wooden loft with rusty shutters, observing the night sky above.

Hidden behind her hood, is a face, that has been aged way too soon… Scars from life's misfortunes written across her cheeks, red lipsticked, stained to chapped lips.

The middle aged lady whispers in rhythms and tantrums, conjuring up spells from long ago, trying to re-create feelings of a hope that was lost so long ago…

In the darkness, a wolf howls its sullen tunes into the silence of the night. The woman in the red-hooded cape awaits for any passersby, waiting for a victim to become her friend.

Again, she speaks in rhymes and waves her hands, hoping to receive good tidings from an accepting friend. The sounds of footsteps making their way through brush and leaves are heard by the woman, as she grows excited with desperation. She turns on a fake sense of charm, her chapped lips growing into a deceitful smile. In the darkness, a wolf howls its sullen tunes into the silence of the night. A shy lonely young girl of perhaps eighteen stops in her tracks, observing her surroundings, realizes that she is lost, and begins to turn the other way…

Although, the woman in the red-hooded cape offers a helping hand, to the misfortune of the shy lonely girl. A wicked smile spreads across the woman's face as she speaks out a fake happy hello, offering help to the lost one…

Unknown to the distraught lady before her, the shy girl walks up to the lady in the red-hooded cape, to see her face better, in the pale glow of the moonlight.

In the darkness, a wolf howls its sullen tunes into the silence of the night. Hidden behind her hood is a face that has been aged way too soon… Scars from life's misfortunes written across her cheeks, red lipsticked, stained to chapped lips.

The young girl, shivers from fear, realizes far too late, a wrong turn has been taken… As the lady in the red-hooded cape embraces her in a hug with a cold loveless touch. A thick smoky fog emerges around the two, and the young girl soon is no more…Instead, a white gray haired wolf scampers away into the darkness, howling sadly into the starless night… While the woman in the red-hooded cape, sits lonely, once again, waiting for an unknown victim to become her friend.

Ariana R. Cherry

The Witchcraft

On a no-moon night
In a pitch-dark jungle
In the middle of nowhere
All the mean witches
Of the world gathered
For an international meet

They wanted to wrest
The control of the world
From the power
Of the kind rulers

Witches arrived
In black overalls
And peaked caps
From all over the world
On different versions of brooms
Made of their local material

There the oldest and the most experienced
Out of them settled down
To prepare a secret potion
That would snatch away
The power of the good
And transfer it to
The power of the evil
So that they could rule the world forever

The witches lit a fire
And placed their magic pot on it
And they poured all kinds of magic potions
And chanted numerous magical words
So that they could become

The most powerful forces on earth…
So that evil can rule over all else in this world

But after hours of brewing
They finally had the secret potion
And, from the secret potion,
Emerged a giant witch…
She was ten times the size
Of other witches
And she ate up all the witches
So that she could have the whole world
To herself and her evil designs

Vincent Van Ross

The Dark Arts

Come hither my child
Do sit a spell
I've got something to tell you
It's foreboding and dark
And right from the start
It depends on your angle of view
Here is the truth
As I can recall
It's hidden inside of a story
There isn't a prince
No dragons are slain
No sign of a hero's glory
But there are goosebumps and goblins
Yeah, they'll give you a fright
And transparent ghosts
Invading the night
Sprites and wild fairies
I'm told they are scary
Live way up high in the trees
A grumpy old troll
And I'm sure that you know
If caught, you'd never break free
The story it goes
Or so I am told
Of a witch who had long been forgotten
She had half a nose
And the evidence shows
The other half gone
Due to the fact it was rotten
An angry old witch
with an iron fist she ruled
Obedience was required
Her subjects were schooled

Poetic Shadows – Ink and the Sword

On how to follow the rules
Afraid to get lost in the mire
That wicked old witch, was not very nice
And a lousy excuse for a master
Then came the day
Let me put it this way
She was struck down by karmic disaster
Beauty it seems
Had been just a dream
Still the object of her desire
She tried books of spells
Cooked unthinkable things
In a cauldron, over the fire

The day of her doom
Came not a minute too soon
The day she looked into the mirror
She remembered a phrase
That ended her days
And it couldn't have been any clearer
Beauty's skin deep
And I'm sure that you know
Ugly goes through to the bone
Those were the words
The whole kingdom heard
As the witch melted into her throne

Lyne Beringer

Threshold

Once, upon a vibrant village,
a scorned sorcerer's spell was cast,
a nebulous cloud covered all;
the masses, throughout, were aghast.
A darkness drenched everyone,
thriving from three thieves' trickery,
as Merlin's disdain doomed dwellers
with his wand's wave of wizardry.
The chain of veiled events began
when the graceful goddess, that ruled,
requested Merlin's treasured stones,
so her steel staff would be bejeweled,
But later, her stave was stolen
by rogues who hid amidst the few,
while the town was blinded by brume,
soon hiding the bandits who knew.
Next, a nomad came to their land,
hooded in black with robe wrapped tight;
each person faced their growing fear,
as every day was the night.
Their terror filled the shrouded soot,
as many suspicions abound
that the stranger was the reason
no one could find the end of town.
Vigilantes searched for the one
who caused their blight and was to blame;
yet, no one could peer past four feet,
and they couldn't keep a lit flame.
Finally, fortune changed their way,
finding the outsider, at last,
but, as they approached, they realized
their fear was from within and vast.
Still, the outcast was now revealed,

Poetic Shadows – Ink and the Sword

as a beacon glowed on the ground.
It was the sacred silver staff
whose new gems glimmered to be found.
Near the inlaid stave lay three bodies,
each overcome by their own greed;
one hard hand still held its handle;
yet, the dim mist punished their deed.
Then, the robe dropped down to the soil,
exposing the one they had feared,
and with the brilliance of the staff,
their fright felt remorse, as eyes teared.
For who stood alone amongst them,
was the one in whom they believed,
and only, from her luminescence,
could their clouded guilt be relieved.
She raised her supreme stave and waved,
as rays beyond the haze appeared.
A gateway opened with fresh air,
so, all those shadowed, could be cleared.
One by one, she escorted them
through the passage into pure light.
They graciously shared her presents
as they journeyed toward golden sight.
Today, they have not forgotten,
for in their lore of young and old,
humbly, they chant, "Just remember
that Goddess through the threshold."

Justin R. Hart

The Man With the Pitchfork

One dark night, I was met on the road
by a man with a pitchfork
who tried to poke me into submission
So, I taught him a lesson or two
Because that's what I do
with my special powers
I gather leaches and flowers,
lavender, the tiny eye of the newt
and a secret ingredient I can't divulge
with a pinch of whatever suits my mood

Oh, they've tried to scare me into compliance
But they have no power without my permission
I inherited a long tradition of willfulness
My freedom takes root in the hedge apple tree
I gather the branches and crush the fruit
underfoot while grinding into the ground
anything they leave lying around
to trick me into being whatever they desire
Then, I throw the remnants upon the fire

The man with the pitchfork was no match for me
He was sent to make sure that I couldn't live free
to run recklessly through the wild woods at night
or with the raven to take sudden flight
That's the kind of thing they can't abide
So they send the pitchforks to tame my spirits
Hoping to subdue my desire to ride
my broomstick under a full moon, I confide

Fear not, my lovelies, I've a coven
of women who were born just like me
with a willful nature and a desire to be free

Poetic Shadows – Ink and the Sword

We gather at night with our familiars
Mixing our potions and chanting our songs
Dancing in circles around the fire
Doing whatever our heart's desire
That's where the man with the pitchfork was taken
That's where he stayed alone and forsaken

So, when you walk through the woods
on a autumn day with the sky so blue
on a gentle foray just remember to look
for the old tree stump with mushrooms
growing that is often mistook
for a harmless seat in the wooded glen
Just beware, my friend — that's him
Oh, yes, my darlings, that's him.

Teresa Roberts

Under the Full Moon

hiking at night
under the full moon
sounds so lovely
the smell of warm stew
drifting on the breeze
seems so inviting
too late you hear
the cackle of laughter
as the net falls upon you
the witches move in
to pull you to the cauldron
the final ingredient in the stew
troll stew, troll stew
they chant again and again
slowing dragging you in
The stock smells delicious
the temperature of a hot tub
maybe I being punk'd after all
no sooner than I relaxed
the fired blazed higher
the water getting too hot
then nothing, nothing at all
now I gaze down upon them
my body still in the cauldron
a bloody hammer in a witch's hand
troll stew, troll stew
they chant on
hiking at night
under the full moon
sounds so lovely

Maggie Mae Carter

The Spell

Over cauldron, brew is moved & slowly stirred,
Eye of newt, entrails of beast & heart of tiny bird,
Hot-pot bubbling, steam with ancient sins arising,
Vows, secrets & rituals of the old hag comprising.

Debated, over mulled & within coven duly mooted,
Solutions, potions, concoctions of herbs deep rooted,
The rites of raven & the old wolf's melancholic tune,
The witch chants & stirs & so turns the ancient moon.

Love for the virgin or long awaited wife for the man,
The wailing & the chanting for a simple change of plan,
The night wind howls & to waiting hell, her song evokes,
Silence reigns, as the spell by the crone is now bespoke.

Beauty bestowed upon the ugly & to rags, new born riches,
Ancient secrets known to none, but only to law of witches,
Death befall upon the heads of neighbors sorry erring,
Night falls, mantled only in the black cat's happy purring.

Sue Lobo

The Lady at the Round Rustic Table

Alone in a dark cool downstairs room, seated around an old rustic round table, sits an elderly woman with long black hair and white highlights woven through.

Her long wrinkled fingers with brittle nails and chipped red polish tap on the old rustic table, as the black candle dances illuminating the dark cool room.

Dressed in a long black red-belted dress, sleeves draping her long thin freckled arms, she sits at the old rustic round table in thought, as she skims an old bound book of spells and long-ago tales, planning a charade for her next victim.

The soft tapping of long wrinkled fingers grows louder, as her sighs become heavier. A quiet cackle escapes dry cracked pink lips, as she humors herself with a plan.

Rising from the old rustic table she hums a mysterious tune and waves her arms swiftly as a white fog enters the room and twirls around her in a slow dance.

Magically, the elderly lady with long black hair is nevermore. A beautiful young busty golden blonde haired maiden dressed in a white red belted gown emerges from the white smog.

Her lips are full, pink and luscious, as she smiles with flirty blue eyes. The black candle's flame extinguishes immediately.

The dark cool room becomes filtered with warmth and sunshine. The young busty maiden runs up the worn creaky stairs, as a quiet cackle escapes her plush pink lips.

Poetic Shadows – Ink and the Sword

Loudly, she laughs and giggles, dancing to the outdoors searching for her next victim. Upon her search, she follows a brick path towards her small hometown village.

A young tall handsome brute with slicked brown hair dressed in his Sunday's suit meets the maiden's blue flirtatious eyes. She bows, giggles and offers a smooth-skinned hand.

As if by magic, the brute is entranced by the maiden's golden beauty. She giggles again, and plants a kiss upon his quivering shocked lips.

A white smog filters through the brick path, and twirls around in a slow dance with the young brute.

Surprised with horror, his youth was stolen unexpectedly. His slicked brown hair now was darkened with white highlights woven through. Long wrinkled fingers and yellowed brittle nails were bestowed upon his aged hands.

A quiet cackle escaped the plush pink lips of the golden maiden. While a hoarse whisper spoke from the old wrinkled brute, "Why?" She giggled out loud and in a sing-song voice yelled, "Good day!" and skipped down the brick path to the small-town village while the brute's youth was nevermore.

Ariana R. Cherry

The Witch of the Woods

The witch of the woods
Armed with black powers,
Hiding under hoods
Of darkness in dark hours;
A human skull in hand
And a marrow bone in another,
To work as a magic wand
As he sneers like a Godfather!

If a traveller has to pass
The woods during this eerie hour,
Seeing the stars on the wet grass,
Feeling the sleeping, fragrant flower;
The witch with his crazy ways
Will scandalize the passerby,
With sinister sounds, untraceable rays,
Vampires grinning in the sky!

He feeds all the innocuous men
With fear and frowns, and smiles
At their helplessness; and then
Thinks of newer tricks and guiles
To lay them in the dusty bed
Of the earth for a final sleep,
Adding number to the dead;
And find more skulls and bones to keep!

Debasish Mishra

Dangerous Love: The Knight And The Witch

How could this be a forbidden love,
So dangerously
Sir Knight willing to die
For the love of his life
As she would do the same
Meeting in their mystical secret
Hiding place leaving no trace
to make magical spells and
Memories that they will
Cherish,
For this they know their love will
Perish,
if his kingdom and the
witches found out
Between the two worlds,
It will be war for sure
They must say good bye
Before their worlds collide
But their love so true,
Neither one can't deny
As the witch says a spell
To spare his broken heart
And kisses his forehead before
they go away they make a promise,
"in my heart you'll stay always".

Tammy S. Thomas

Liberating Luminance

In distant times of darkened light,
a wiling witch once bewildered
and hence, entranced two unicorns,
a meek, meandering mother
and her sole, unsuspecting son.
Her trance transformed her own image
to a vestal virtue virgin
of whom would hastily attract
the innocence of unicorns.
Thereupon, the mother approached
the spellbinder's feigned luminance.
She soon laid her neck, naively,
on the mage's maternal lap.
As the sorceress stroked her head,
the spell's glare and lustre lessened.
It suddenly seemed a true gleam,
brighter from above, also beamed,
and as the candescence came down,
its shining shafts swiftly shattered
the delusion of illusion,
and unto those radiant rays,
Purity peerlessly appeared,
an angel full of effulgence
and brilliance broke the spent spell.
Yet, just in mere mournful moments,
it took one swift swipe of her knife
before the chilling enchantress
could cut off the unicorn's horn,
the one missing ingredient
for her purifying potion
to be bartered to the bishop.
Thereafter, the mother's essence
faded, with her spiraling spirit,

disappearing in a mystic mist.
Still, the time was most imminent
to complete the angel's journey
to rescue the young unicorn,
whom, while reigned by rope, was soon led
to a sacred sanctuary.
As she spoke in a subdued voice
only he could heartily hear,
she assured with the faithful phrase:
"Let Purity illuminate
and graciously guide your forged fate;
leave darkness behind shadow's gait."

Justin R. Hart

Witches

The moon is endowed with mood enhancers
Its luminosity powerfully affecting the tides
My madness of moods surges with the waves,
the witch on the broomstick taking a ride.

Don't mock my kindred spirits or me
I do not conjure such moody blues
But recognize the pull in my solar plexus
It's a gift that I did not choose.

Wild is the ride, the pull irresistible
The scent of the wind, the call for her child
Mother Nature daring us to ride, ride, ride
We embrace our roots, totally beguiled.

And, yes, there was a time when my kind
were burned at the stake, restrained from flying
But we surprised them all with our tenacity
Calling upon the moon even as we were dying.

The moon is the light that beckons me
Translucently soft but ferociously divine
She's the wand in the hand of my mother force,
the song of the minstrel so fine.

Long ago, I relinquished the need to resist
Gathering my skirts, I gave the moon a sweet kiss
And when she rises to rule the blue seas
I bow to her power on my bended knees.

We witches are what we were intended to be
In love with the moon — wild and free.

Teresa Roberts

Poetic Shadows – Ink and the Sword

Epilogue

Publishing Assistance

In 2013 Ms. Raja Williams realized that there was a gap, a void if you will, within the publishing industry. A writer either had to come up with hundreds, sometimes thousands of dollars to release a book or take on the journey of self-publishing alone. There was no middle ground, no one there to assist, either financially or lead the way in self-publishing. Most writers do not have the finances to pay a publisher, and some don't know where to start when it comes to self-publishing, nor are they prepared to be in business for themselves.

Raja was inspired to start a fund to assist writers in becoming published authors at either a discounted rate or a full publishing scholarship. To begin this fund Raja paid for the publishing of our first anthology Love, a Four Letter Word. Comprised of poets from all around the world. The sales generated from the purchases of the book were placed into a fund that enabled us to fund future publishing's.

We now are able to offer anthology publications, a chance for authors to have a voice in the literary world yearly, and we have been able to offer several authors full scholarships, as well as offering deep discounted publishing services as a whole. We are thankful for the continued support of this program by both our readers and writers alike.

For More Information Please Visit Our Website At:

www.ctupublishinggroup.com/starving-artist-fund.html

Creative Talents Unleashed

Get Connected With Us!

Website: Creative Talents Unleashed Publishing Group

www.ctupublishinggroup.com

Facebook: Get connected with us on our Facebook Page

www.Facebook.com/Creativetalentsunleashed

Twitter: https://twitter.com/CTUPublishing

Blog: www.creativetalentunleashed.com

Pinterest: https://www.pinterest.com/creativetalents/

Instagram: https://instagram.com/ctupublishinggroup/

Tumblr: http://creativetalentsunleashed.tumblr.com/

Creative Talents Unleashed

Creative Talents Unleashed is an independent publishing group that offers writers an opportunity to share their writing talents with the world. We are committed to fostering and honoring the work of writers of all cultures. Our publishing group offers writing tips to assist writers in continued growth and learning, daily writing prompts and challenges to keep the writers mind sharp and challenged, marketing and events, as well as a variety of yearly publishing opportunities. We are honored to be assisting writers in the journey of becoming published authors.

www.ctupublishinggroup.com

For More Information Contact:

Creativetalentsunleashed@aol.com

www.ingramcontent.com/pod-product-compliance
Lightning Source LLC
Chambersburg PA
CBHW071302040426
42444CB00009B/1838